Tell Me
When You Get There

poems by

Lia Rivamonte

Finishing Line Press
Georgetown, Kentucky

Tell Me When You Get There

Copyright © 2019 by Lia Rivamonte
ISBN 978-1-63534-975-7 First Edition
All rights reserved under International and Pan-American Copyright Conventions. No part of this book may be reproduced in any manner whatsoever without written permission from the publisher, except in the case of brief quotations embodied in critical articles and reviews.

ACKNOWLEDGMENTS

This book would not be possible without the support of my family and friends but especially: the Bayless Avenue Poets—Barbara Davis, Alice O. Duggan, MaryAnn Franta Moenck, and Paige Riehl for continued sustenance with a special shout out to Carolyn Williams-Noren for her time and insights, and Naomi Cohn for her persistent, but good-natured encouragement; to Ann Bauleke for thoughtful editorial assistance, and to Dan Fernelius for his creativity and enthusiasm. I am indebted to Kirsten Dierking and Margaret Hasse for their generous reading, and to mentor, provocateur, and constant source of inspiration, David Mura, who ensures that the voices of Asian American writers are heard. To my siblings—Milly Looby, Loudi, Ramon, and Joaquin Rivamonte and to my smart, funny, beautiful children—Andrei and Sophie Kissin, Sophie Kissin, and their dad, Michael Kissin and bonus children, Henry Brown and Lydia Hinton, thank you for being. Thank you to the Metropolitan Regional Arts Council Next Step grant program for understanding the need for travel.

And finally, to my husband, Matt Brown—for without his steadfast love and support I would be rudderless.

Publisher: Leah Maines
Editor: Christen Kincaid
Cover Art: Dan Fernelius and Lia Rivamonte
Author Photo: Dan Fernelius
Cover Design: Dan Fernelius

Printed in the USA on acid-free paper.
Order online: www.finishinglinepress.com
also available on amazon.com

Author inquiries and mail orders:
Finishing Line Press
P. O. Box 1626
Georgetown, Kentucky 40324
U. S. A.

Table of Contents

And There They Were 1

Praise Song For Our Mothers 2

Lumpia is the Food of the Gods 3

After Bataan 5

Canuto & Helen 6

What I Might Have Dreamed 8

Pleats 9

Lullaby 10

Elegy 11

Summer Night, and the River 12

People Are Sleeping 14

The Color of Shame 15

Zhou Dang and the Boatman 16

lie down 18

Meatloaf 19

Half-Listening to NPR Can Be Haazardous to Your Health 20

Ordinary Singing 21

Notes on Building a Relationship with Customers 22

Atonement, Again 23

Slippery Dream or How She Imagined Transformation and
    Lost Her Nerve 26

Humble Being 28

Immanence 29

Tell Me When You Get There 30

For Carlos and Lou, ever present, ever loved.

And There They Were

He in his *barong tagalog*
and wide, cunning grin, her
fraudulent shy one, butterfly
sleeves and lashes aflutter, a drawer
full of gifts from suitors fortifying
the audacity of her sly glance.
He had straight teeth, wavy
hair, wire-rimmed spectacles belying
his cheekiness, two children
and a dead wife—a complex
of scars running beneath
his embroidered finery. Her girlfriends
hushed as he brushed past, pulled
as if by an unseen thread toward her ripe
mouth, and ivory skin. (Thank god
she'd heeded Mama's repeated
exhortations to *cover up*.) Her heart
pumping, blood flowing
too fast behind her eyes, filling
up her ears as she parted her lips
to ask—as if she hadn't already
known—his name and following
that, the dizzying anticipation
of her name on his tongue like
some sweet song. He couldn't sing
a note and stepped on her feet.
Nevertheless, they danced
for a long, long time.

Praise Song for Our Mothers

Praise be to the mother of Lapulapu Dimantag,
Datu of Mactan who led his men bearing
bamboo spears into victorious battle against
Magellan and his company of armored marauders.
Praise be to the Datu, known by many names: Çilapulapu,
Si Lapulapu, Salip Pulaka, Cali Pulaco—Resistor
of Religion, Gold, and other such Stuff.
Those things are worthless, said his mother. Open your eyes—
here is a bounty of emerald coconuts, diamond waters and above
us, skies of lapis, sapphire, and turquoise.
He nodded, this was true.
What should we make of those Italian sailors
who joined the Spaniards and Portuguese desperate
or foolhardy, debarked from four-masted galleons, claimed
our land and renamed us failing to understand
we had no need of Baptism—the progeny of rapists,
adventurists, and scalawags—our mothers made us pure.

Lumpia is the Food of the Gods

Make them like this: blend
flour and water in a medium-sized
bowl for a thin batter, heat
a well-seasoned iron skillet, dip
a corner of paper towel into
the mix, and use it like a paint
brush—swirl the batter into the center
of the pan with a delicate twist of
the wrist in a circular motion
to form a wafer-like skin. In a few
moments, you will lift this skin off
the bed of the pan, and hold
it up to the light by its laced edge
so your mother can see you through
it from wherever she is, to make
sure you are doing it exactly as
she had done at her stove in
the camp amid the orange groves
with Japanese and Mexican and Filipino
kids looking on, knot of hunger
growing heavy in their bellies.

Place the finished wrapper on waxed
paper, stacking each fragile, transparent
circle on top of the other careful
not to let them stick together. Now the
the filling: julienne a head of cabbage
(Napa is best), sauté two pounds of ground
pork, with fine-chopped onions and
garlic, toss in a cup of garbanzos, add
the cabbage, salt, pepper, and soya to taste,
fold a handful of crisp bean sprouts
in at the last. Spoon a small mound
of this mixture onto a fresh wrapper, roll
it up into a tight, fat cigar—don't forget

to moisten your fingertips with water
to smooth them over the edges of the roll
to seal. Before frying in hot peanut oil put
aside a few uncooked for the children
who stand at your elbow, just as you stood
at your mother's side to glare
at the children who watched
your mother cook,
for you were hungry, too.

After Bataan

Grampa tended roses.
Enormous perianth curls swollen with color—
yellow, deep burgundy, pink, their pale
trunks naked and upright. He tied
their errant arms to stakes laid
out in perfect circles of pebbled dirt,
appraising each—snipping, standing,
crouching, snipping—pinching
soil between thumb and forefinger,
dancing a prim minuet between each bush.
Nothing in his tendering spoke
of the brutality: grim slog on a road
tripping over dead, sixty-eight miles
under a shroud of heavy yellow
heat, prodded by bayonets,
stench of rotted flesh betraying
the perfume of ditch blooms.
Only silence as he plied each petal
transfixed by its soft indifference.

Canuto & Helen

Held by the arms
of a big green chair

he sucks his pipe, smoke
rising in wisps,

eyes fixed
on the football bleeding

red as it arcs across
the TV screen.

In heavy powder, dead
fox dangling

along her copious
chest, she stands outside

waits for the bus to bridge
club. His dinner under

the dishtowel: lima
beans, rice, roast beef, cherry pie.

She prefers tomato aspic atop
a bed of iceberg

lettuce. He is home
after years at war.

This truce was signed
a long time ago.

What I Might Have Dreamed

I might have dreamed of Danny's funeral, his burial wagon backlit
by a silver sun at noon with tin embossing of fleurs-de-lys, and

tulips on the rooftop pointing towards the sky. I might have dreamed
of the church where the priest intones

prayers, congregants sing hymns of love and joy, and in the yard,
the march of mourners begin their hushed walk under a hot, hot

sun to the miniature city of whitewashed graves on the edge
of town. Or maybe I dreamed of parasols and drugstores, of pretty

girls in uniforms, guards and boys who love unbidden, of coconuts
and mountain goats, daughters with children, of mothers holding

tight to purses, and the fathers who limp behind. These dreams of an
island with copper mines, unspoiled rivers, priests named Merlin,

of Harley, Lovely, and Darling—these are the things I might have
dreamed—these are the things I want for you.

Pleats

Sunday nights after laundering, the wool
of our skirts is fragrant with powdered
Oxydol. We iron them warm—the red
and green plaid—the ones we must wear
from sixth grade on because the earlier
style jumpers pull too taut over
our bumptious chests. The pleats take
time to press: hold down three
at once, make sure there is water
in the iron for steam or the folds
will spring back up—unruly proof
of our intransigent souls. (Jeanie Haley
and Cindy Williams have straight fine
hair, the white polish on their shoes
never shines to gray, is always white,
their pleats align, stay flat with
knife-sharp creases.) By Friday,
my skirt will be stiff with Thursday's hot
chocolate; the pleats embedded with gravel
and tar, a little blood, sloughed off
skin, tears, and sweat—the flesh of a girl.

Lullaby

I , I, I, I,
sing don't cry
cielito lindo
I wish I could tell you
in Spanish my heart
to your heart-shaped
face the earth is shaking
the oceans grow
warm yet you and I
are trembling your wide
dark eyes your widow's peak
from grandma
O as if the earth is trying
to shake the stupid
men and women off
and now has stopped
its spin to still
the beautiful notes
of this song
ay ay ay ay
little darling our
dreams
are dying I
wish I could
sing to you
in Spanish strum
my heart-shaped
guitar ay ay ay ay like
the sky cries
sing

Elegy
> *for Carl*

Honey bees are dying, the orchards lie in waste.
In spring, cream, brown-headed larvae tunnel

through open wounds in the bark of the apricots bleeding
sap and frass, as bees writhe at the foot of the trees.

Decades since our brother worked those orchards picking
the fruit, his rebel tendencies camouflaged

among tree trunks and our cousins, all brown,
all lean. In the driveway, he stands against a car squinting

to block the sun or an over-bright moon, or stars imploding,
his limbs thrum, he flips a cig at the camera lens.

The bees' furred bodies in the brittle grass
leak an amber fluid not sweet like honey but twangy

and thin—at least that's what I imagine—I should open
my browser and find out the facts about those stars

and what they are made of.

Summer Night, and the River

At dusk she pushed the stroller
to the high curve

of the bridge, waiting
for the crowds to disperse—

she'd forgotten about the holiday.

As the last of the rockets broke
open, spilling color against

the dark sky, sending slivers of light
to skitter and dance across

the river-glass, across the taut, smooth skin
of her arms across her body

weightless, his body, too.
No splash as the baby burst

through the pliant skin of the river—
that part in the air

took longer than she imagined
his pink-gummed smile

landing on the pillow
of sand, deep, deep.

How cold was the water
if it was cold. The other

boy reached for his mama's
hand, squeezed it tight, eyes glowing

violet, his nails cutting
into her palm—summer heat

pressing into her temples. On
her knees, she drew him

close, his breath seared
her forehead branding

it *love*, she whispered or maybe
sweet jesus, as she

lifted him up over the railing
and let go.

People are Sleeping

In the open, nothing
to eat, nowhere to defecate or bleed

in private. We want the composer to make
sounds that envelope our sadness with a cool

fog of noise, smoothing
the clenched knot of witness

with uplifting chords. Come sleep
with us—our beds lie empty, our closets full—

oh, yes and there's cable
TV, prosciutto, and Häagen-Dazs.

Notes trickle down the mountainside,
chords diminish, evaporate into dust,

families are rent, and all the light is trapped
beneath the ruined mosque. Pop tunes rise

from the arena stage but no one feels
like dancing. We nod off,

eager for our vacant dreams
to end and after, birdsong.

The Color of Shame
    (On listening to the poet Bao Phi on the radio)

Covering a lush, therefore, inappropriate
green with primer, I am listening
to a poet on the radio
talk about his complicity
thinking about what it means
and all those times I conspired
with unseen perpetrators to unleash
that slow-spreading poison.
The poet speaks
of the embarrassment he felt
for his immigrant father, watching
him repair a broken fence—
damage wrought by neighboring
hate-vandals. That feeling of betrayal:
by skin color
accent
texture
hair
shape of eyes, nose, lips, dress, music
the permanent perfume
of soy sauce and baskets—yes
shame.
Laughed with others knowing
that buzzing inside my ears
the heat swelling behind my eyes
was nothing more, nothing less.
I glide my paint-loaded brush over
dark-stained walls—it takes two coats—
the first is neutral, unassuming;
the second, light and inoffensive.
Higher I climb up the ladder to reach
the ceiling, hoping to achieve
just the right shade of yellow.

Zhou Dang and the Boatman
After a painting by Li San

1
Zhou Dang squints at the river from his shelter
on the mountainside to see
the rushing water washing
over rock, jags of light sliding,
slipping into shadow, the lotus
blossoms rising, falling
with the current.
He lifts his brush, touches
its tip to the surface of the paper, observes
as the black ink runs, seeps into the pale-dry
fibers; he smiles under his wisp-beard, or
is that a grimace as he tries to capture
the flowing waters, the flowers'
respiration?
No one disturbs the silk
shoulder of his jacket
with a light hand
to say the tea is ready;
he is parched. Downriver,
a man in a boat plays
the flute, the notes of a song
only the birds can recognize.

2
The artist, Li San, meditates on his subject:
Zhou Dang Gazing Out Over the Lotus Flowers.
He begins with the roof: each tile a solid
rectangle, each edge equal to the next, then
the water: sweeping his ink-loaded brush, swift
stroke after swift stroke. Do not think, move
your wrist, flick the ink, breathe as you
move; make a rhythm of your curves, there
one lotus, here, another. In one hundred
years—in two—they will know your elegant

brushwork, they will tell how Li San made
the water sing like the boatman sings
with his flute; there, you draw a simple
boatman blowing into his hollowed
reed, his notes in perfect harmony
with the water.

lie down

sleep
if this isn't coming
count your wrinkles
the ones crawling around and up your thighs
sing a low hymn
the one that comes just after the homily
when the sun pouring in through leaded windows
stripes your bare arms, trickles between follicles
highlights your husband's dusky finger tips
the ones that seek refuge
in the loose folds of flesh
lining your belly and lower still
think of the wind
the kind that gusts at your back
lifts the hem of your blouse
flattens the stray wisps lacing
your temples let
your eyelashes tremble, the fine muscles
of your upper cheek slacken
settle your tongue behind the teeth
hold the urge to swallow—
that bird wants to fly—
now hold its warm, throbbing
body close for a good thirty seconds
let it go

Meatloaf

When father throws
the meatloaf against the brick
wall the children may wonder:
Is everything going to be okay?
They are hungry
for meals
that aren't smashed
but aligned
on their plates in separate
mounds, better to see
what it is.
Not to be surprised
at spicy or sweet,
too hot, or too
cold. We all want
to know: will it burn
my tongue? Why does it smell
like the earth
that clings to the bottom
of a mushroom?
Is it rough like bark on a pine?
Or will it glide
through my sluice-throat
smooth as a marble
leaving no splinters—
no need to recall
what it was.
As adults we crave
the comfort of knowing
our tongues
will not betray
us, that our principles
are founded on the truth
of who we are—
that is, what we eat.

Half-Listening to NPR Can Be Hazardous to Your Health

The consequences will not be soft—
not like the down on the swan's
underneck or the newly-born's
fontanel floating in warm belly
liquid, the dad sitting
on the bench watching
softball; there, détente, here
a reckoning, my gut saying
by all means do it and yet
his breath all Ketel One—clear,
present, dangerous. We refuse
to look away from those eyes,
baby, those eyes. You can't be for real,
we say, but he is. (Why are there any planets
at all if we can't visit without paying
an arm and a leg and a few more pair?)
Professor, you call yourself learned
but what you know is locked
away in a jelly jar on the shelf
in Aunt Milma's basement,
inert, unsterile, sullied. Like
all other facts, dirt.

Ordinary Singing

That pain—where did it come from?

Horns, strings, bassoons—they have to change
     weights somewhere. We've seen enough movies
to know it won't end well.   Ducks float
on plush bottoms (so many things to note with binoculars)
     like the underbelly of this music—
an oboe, reeds, rushes, and   that voice.

Flags quiver, behind them   flotilla of clouds.
     French horns drag her deeper
         into
            sickness
the cancer migrates
     through the archipelago—so many unsafe harbors
        now another trill—
how do you describe the voice of the ecstatic?

Tell me more—we want to hear—like watching
a boat moving along   the inevitable current
    and taking with it
        the whole shebang.

Notes on Building a Relationship with Customers

The quality of the conversation
is the important thing. The red
envelope, the catalog, red wrapping
paper, ribbon—that's commitment.
Make them smile (not necessarily online).
Free gifts   free phone calls
are portable, repeatable, emotional.
Word of mouth
has measurable results.
Google maps, traffic reports—keep
the conversation going. Be the purple
cow—help your fans tell
their friends how terrific
you are. New love is powerful. Nobody
talks more than a scorned lover.

Would anybody tell a friend about you?

Remember, it's what you share
not where you share it. The reason
to talk might be something other
than what you think.

(Try lots of little things. *Experiment*
then throw your weight
behind that.)

Atonement, Again

1

Why is it each year the season of atonement
is so beautifully colored? Soft-edged
like an ordinary snapshot made into art
as you click through the handy filters
on your phone: glow, antique, neon.

2

I can't forgive myself for wanting more
and more, every day more. I am surrounded
by addiction, the habit of need.

3

For an instant we stand under falling
gold butterflies and believe in their abundance,
imagine a future of lovely piles, burnished
leaves on the green banks of deep
ponds mirroring a cloudless sky.

4

I hate myself for looking into my brother's eyes
and feeling nothing.

5

It is his birthday, born two weeks after
another brother died. I am ashamed for screaming,

for losing my cool when he tells us we are doing it all wrong:
be careful of that paper, don't lose that book, hey that's my music.

6

He wants to talk about that time when…, that girl he…
Every few minutes he leaves the room to pour
another. He won't drink in front of us; he is in control.

7

In the parking lot, we lean against the car, worry and joke,
our bodies depleted from lifting and sorting, pleading
and exhorting, unable to avoid inhaling
billowing clouds of weed.

8

A few summers ago, I spied him walking up the street
to our mother's house wearing a long wool coat, a jaunty,
brimmed hat—cheerful old man making his way home
from the liquor store. Only he isn't old, but skipped
past his prime, racing towards rot.

9

A thick row of persimmon trees lines the walk
to his door. I pluck the unripe fruit, even snap
off a branch of hard green knobs, toss it all
into the back of my rental
car. Once, not far from this place, a boy
I liked dropped a pulpy, orange-gold
fruit into my lap—since then *persimmons*

is a favorite idea.

I abandon the fruit and the branch at the airport.

10

I call my brother who is still sitting
in the middle of the room we emptied
out a month ago. He is being evicted,
vows to resist this evisceration; his
apartment is his body— we are tearing
him apart, he says. I say *hand over the keys.*

Slippery Dream or How She Imagined Transformation and Lost Her Nerve

There's a place in Sedona where
women float, imagining the sea
as they lie under plexi-glass

domes high above red rocks. Flipping
from belly onto backside, eyes flutter
closed, they swim into an ocean

of sound emitted through
speakers—squeaking, clicking,
crying—the echo-locative language

of dolphins. Only one
woman struggles, resisting
the call to soften, squeezing

her muscles tight while the others
slacken, exhale through blowholes—push
push, pushing out their stale,

used air. For them nothing old remains:
organs re-form beneath sheathed
blubber, bones fuse

into flippers and fins until
finally, these newborn
dolphins lift, fly

up into salt-spray,
leaving the woman to sink
in their wake. She returns

home, makes dinner, walks
the dog; her body still freighted
with a woman's flesh—heavy

matter—bound to the earth
as she treads over the ice,
and tries not to slip.

Humble Being

Here you are mid-flight
not at all wondering—no need
to contemplate like we of mud,
bone, and red blood. When you
don't have to love you repeat
the patterns and never tire. Dying
is not a tragedy it's just what
happens. Your blues
the backdrop, not an invitation
to suffer. Each breath brings
us closer to annihilation, your
oblivion. The gold-clad
chrysanthemum, all the flowers
in the garden wait, open,
wave. They couldn't care
less about husbands.

Immanence

said the old man,
Now, go and talk about It.
There is peace before disaster,
peace before violence, but only
because you have to stop
and reload. I've seen my share
of westerns, gangster, war,
and spy movies. I've studied
the faces of the killed, the killer,
their mothers. Every mouth
trembles whether from fear
or lust, every hand icy, stiff
with longing or death, every
heart stops, the noise deafening.
It's not so serious, you laugh,
but like the old man said.

Tell Me When You Get There

Let me know if you find yourself bumping
along the freeway, tires flat, out
of gas or brake fluid or heat. In
the old days, your horse might have thrown
you, left you stranded roadside, ass sore
from the hard leather saddle dependent
on a nasty stranger with a handlebar
mustache—heck he might be sitting
at the truck stop counter swilling
black coffee eying your doughnut.
Let me know if the couch you sleep
on is gritty, the shower spray needlelike
softening your suffering lumbar. (You're
the one refused my beaded backrest.)
When you arrive, text me. Say
you heart me, didn't mean to leave
me forever and have saved me
a place by the fire.

Lia Rivamonte was born and raised in the S.F. Bay Area, but has lived in Minnesota since the 1980's. She graduated from U.C. Berkeley with a BA in Art, worked for several years in professional theatre and received a MFA in Painting at the University of Minnesota. She has served as executive director for Banfill-Locke Center for the Arts, and currently works in fundraising and development for Mixed Blood Theatre Company in Minneapolis. Since participating in a Loft Literary Center mentorship program in the mid 90's, she has been writing on and off—plays, short fiction, and poetry. She was awarded an Artist Initiative grant from the Minnesota State Arts Board grant in 2014 and a Next Step grant from the Metropolitan Regional Arts Council the following year to support a long fiction project on which she continues to labor. A second generation Filipino American, much of her writing explores her Filipino roots and the stories of her immigrant grandparents—real and imagined.

She lives with her husband in the Little Bohemia neighborhood of St. Paul, Minnesota.

www.ingramcontent.com/pod-product-compliance
Lightning Source LLC
LaVergne TN
LVHW041509070426
835507LV00012B/1428